CONTENTS

COVER PHOTO BY KEITH MORRISON
INSIDE COVER PHOTO BY BILL MOORE

Foreword

June 2013

This is not a dictionary, just a selection of Shetland dialect words and phrases on different subjects: weather, food, place-names, the sea, the coastline, etc., together with added information and plenty of photographs. The lists are not exclusive; plenty of other words exist.

The book may be useful to you if you are visiting Shetland, or have come to live here, or if you have an interest in words and languages. We hope it will entertain as well as explain.

If you belong to Shetland, it may be a book you would like to own, for fun. It should offer you scope for some good discussion and get you thinking about words!

Please forgive us if any of your own favourite words and expressions are not included; it's not a big book.

Shetland ForWirds is a voluntary organisation which aims to promote and encourage the continued use of the Shetland dialect. Our grateful thanks to Doreen Waugh, who has led the *Mirds o Wirds* project from the start, and has painstakingly compiled and edited the information and written much of the text, with some help and contributions from Mary Blance, Derick Herning, myself, Nat Hall and Bill Moore.

Laureen Johnson
Shetland ForWirds convener,
2008-2013

Forewird

June 2013

Dis is no a dictionary. Wir waled oot a lock o Shetland wirds an phrases aboot things laek wadder, maet, place-names, da sea, da costline, an sae on, an pitten in information an plenty o photos. Mind, der nae want o idder wirds at we could a pickit forbye dis eens.

You might fin dis book useful if you're veesitin Shetland, or you're come here ta bide, or if you're interested in wirds an languages. We hoop you'll fin it lightsome readin as weel as laernin fae it.

If you belang ta Shetland, dis is maybe a book at you wid laek ta own for a fun. Hit sood get you tinkin aboot wirds, an you sood fin things ta spaek aboot an traep ower!

Dunna hadd it against wis if ony o your ain favourite wirds an sayins is no here; hit's a peerie book.

Shetland ForWirds is a group o volunteers at's set oot ta promote da Shetland dialect an help ta keep it in fok's minds. Doreen Waugh is steered wir *Mirds o Wirds* project fae da start, an we canna tank her enyoch; she's taen great pains in pittin da information tagidder an she's written da maest o da text, wi a grain o help an contributions fae Mary Blance, Derick Herning, mesel, Nat Hall an Bill Moore.

Laureen Johnson
Shetland ForWirds convener,
2008-2013

The island of Colsay and Muckle Sound, near Scousburgh. NH

Shetland

indicating the main inhabited islands

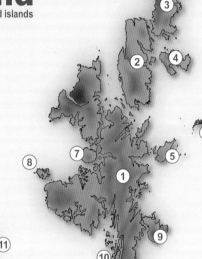

1. MAINLAND
2. YELL
3. UNST
4. FETLAR
5. WHALSAY
6. OUT SKERRIES
7. MUCKLE ROE
8. PAPA STOUR
9. BRESSAY
10. TRONDRA & BURRA
11. FOULA
12. FAIR ISLE

Introduction

The dialect of the Shetland Islands is a descendant of the Scots tongue spoken by the Lowlanders who settled here after Shetland was put in pawn to the Scottish crown by Christian I of Denmark/Norway. As the Scottish grip tightened, more and more of the Norn-speaking inhabitants found it expedient or necessary to acquire a good working knowledge of Scots. Gradually the Norn language, which had now lost its legal status, became restricted to the home and croft. By the end of the 18th century it was virtually extinct in Shetland. Meanwhile the Scots tongue spoken here had absorbed a plethora of words and phrases from native Shetlanders, bolstered by the vocabulary which had already been borrowed into Lowland Scots from the Danelaw in England. The Dutch fishermen who began to visit our waters in the 16th century, and continued to do so until the outbreak of World War I, also contributed words and phrases. The modern Shetland dialect is thus a rich hybrid; principally Scots but clearly showing Scandinavian influence in vocabulary, grammar and pronunciation.

West Sandwick beach, Yell. KM

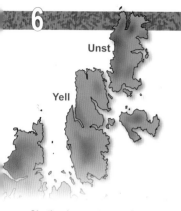

Unst

Yell

'**ö**'

is a common Shetland vowel sound

short, as in
  shön (shoes)
  röf (roof)

long, as in
  campin böd
  crö (sheep-pen)
  Muckle Rö (island)

Ask for demonstrations!

Shetland accents vary from area to area. We only have space to mention a few of the differences here.

The most common difference is between:

AA and AU (which sounds *aw*) as in:
  taaties / tauties (potatoes)
  saat / saut (salt)

AU is common in **Yell and Unst**, and also through the **South Mainland**. AA is more prevalent throughout the rest of Shetland.

Da Wastside (The Westside) This is the name given not to the whole western seaboard of Shetland but to the fist of land which juts out westwards from the Central Mainland of Shetland.

On Da Wastside:
ö is pronounced ö-ee
Initial wh- becomes qu-
  white / quite
  e.g. a quite car

People elsewhere in Shetland sometimes do this in reverse!
  Da Queen / Da Wheen
  A quarry / a wharrie

South Mainland

Da Wastside

Whalsay

Whalsay is often noted for its
distinctive vowel sounds, some of
which are shared by Fair Isle,
e.g:

e as in men, bed
becomes a diphthong
something like
may-in, bay-id

ay as in day
becomes something like oi

This is a sound which the rest of
Shetland finds difficult to say / soi!

Place-names ending in *-wick* on
the map may be pronounced in
one of three different ways. It is
wise to ask if you are not sure!

Example: Lerwick.

Depending on where in
Shetland people belong, they
may say Ler**WEEK**, Ler**ICK**, or
Ler**OOK**. (The 'Lerook' variation
is a feature of north mainland
speech.)

'Eshaness' is pronounced
*Aish*ness, with the stress on
Aish-, not on *-ness*.

The word '*geo*', (page
56/57) appears frequently in
coastline names on maps. It is
pronounced with a **hard 'g'**. It is
NOT '*Gee-o*'!

Alternative spellings are '*gio*',
'*gyo*' or '*gjo*'.

*Stirlings lookin fir
a winter feed. NH*

Some common Shetland Birds

This bird, commonly known as the Great Skua in English, returns every year to breed in Shetland. It looks like a large brown **maa** (gull) with white flashes near the ends of its wings. The **bonxie** is a vicious predator, attacking other birds and stealing their food. It frequently attacks **solans** (gannets) as they return with fish to their nests. It can kill other birds, even if they are larger than it. Do not go near the nest of a **bonxie**. If you do, you may get a **baff** or a **dunt** (blow) on the head as it flies over you!

Bonxie or Skooi (Great Skua). NH

Bonxie (Great Skua) in flight – a menacing sight. NH

The **solan** (gannet) is Shetland's largest breeding bird. The adult has **snaa-white fedders** (snow-white plumage), a yellow head and black wing tips. It can plunge from a great height into the sea to catch fish. It frequently falls prey to the **bonxie**. On the island of Noss there is one of the largest colonies of **solans** in Europe.

Solan (Gannet). NH

Dunter (Eider). NH

The **dunter** is a large, thickset sea **deuk** (duck). The drake's colours, seen here, are mainly black and white with some green on the head, while the female is dark brown. The nest can be built just above the tide-line or further inland, and consists of a scrape which the female lines with her own breast **fedders** (feathers). **Maas** and **bonxies** predate this attractive bird and its numbers are declining.

The **maalie** (fulmar) is a thickset grey and white bird, like a stiff-winged gull. However, its nostrils, encased in tubes, indicate that it is a distant relative of the albatross. **Maalies** first nested in Foula in 1876 but now nest everywhere along the coastline of the British Isles. When sitting on its nest, the **maalie** will spew out an evil-smelling oil to deter intruders. This bird can live for up to fifty years!

Maalie (Fulmar). NH

The **shalder** – "da fool wi da rid neb"** (the bird with the red beak) – is a familiar sight in Shetland. The smart black and white plumage and red bill make it easy to identify. It uses its long beak to dislodge **lempets** (limpets) from seashore rocks and to open shellfish. Nowadays you can also see **shalders** grubbing for worms etc. in fields. Most fly south **i da hairst** (in the autumn) but a few stay on in the Shetland Mainland. These might, however, be Faroese **shalders** which choose to winter here.

Shalder (Oystercatcher). NH

Tammie Norie (Puffin). NH

The **tammie norie** is an attractive **peerie** bird, black above and white below. In the breeding season it has a large **neb** (beak) in three vivid colours, most of which it loses in the winter. In recent years, the **tammie norie**, like some other birds, has suffered from a lack of suitable food (mainly sandeel with which it feeds its young) and its numbers have plummeted.

Anidder Tammie Norie (another Puffin) – the favourite of many visitors to Shetland. NH

Tirrick (Arctic Tern) in flight – a beautiful sight. NH

*A **stirling** (left) and a **blackie** (right) – both these birds are common in Shetland. NH*

Horse-gock or snippick (Snipe). NH

The **horse-gock's** plumage is in various shades of brown and it has a long, slender **neb**. It is a secretive bird and feeds among **lang girse** (long grass) or **floss** (rushes). When disturbed, it flies away at the very last minute with a zigzag flight. In the breeding season, the male swoops down from a height to make a drumming noise with his extended tail feathers, perhaps reminiscent of the sound of a horse **nickerin** (whinnying) and hence the name **horse-gock** or horse-cuckoo. This is a territorial display. The alternative name, **snippick,** is a diminutive of snipe.

Laverock (Lark). NH

The **laverock** is the small bird you will hear **i da voar** (in the spring) and **simmer** (summer) as it **laavs** (hovers) so far up **i da lift** (in the sky) that you can barely see it, and the male pours out his extraordinary love song **da lee-lang day** (all day long). This delightful songster nests on moorland and arable land and flies south **i da hairst** (in the autumn). Many Shetlanders just use the English word **skylark**, but all would understand Scots **laverock**.

Rain-gös *(Rain-goose or red throated diver). NH*

**When da rain-gös gengs ta da sea,
Draw up your boats anunder da lea.
But when da rain-gös gengs ta da hill,
Draw doon your boats an geng whaar you will.**

(When the rain-goose goes to the sea, draw up your boats in a sheltered spot. But when the rain-goose goes to the hill, draw down your boats and go wherever you will.) This piece of folklore is widely known, but the verse given here is from Nicolson, J.R., *Traditional Life in Shetland*

The **rain-gös** has a chestnut-brown throat in the breeding season. On a map of Shetland you will find, here and there, the name **Loomishun** which, in the old Norn language means 'loch or tarn of the rain-gös', telling us that this diving bird has probably bred in the same spot for hundreds of years. **I da voar** (in the spring) it has a long-drawn-out, wailing cry. It loses its throat colour in winter but can be identified by its slightly upturned **neb** (beak).

Robbie Cuddie (Shetland Wren). NH

The **Robbie Cuddie**, as the wren is known in some parts of Shetland, is the islands' smallest resident breeding bird. Its song is surprisingly loud and can be heard throughout the year. Its dark, rusty brown **fedders** (feathers) and cocky tail make it unmistakable. The Shetland wren is darker and larger than the Scottish wren and it is considered to be a subspecies.

Staneshakker, Chak or Stinkle, etc. (Wheatear). NH

The wheatear has several dialect names in Shetland, as below, or variants of these. It is a common breeding bird and remains here from April to September. Both the male and the female have a striking black and white tail pattern. **I da simmer** (in the summer) the male has a grey back which turns buff **i da hairst** (in the autumn). The female has a buff back and brownish wings. The **staneshakker** nests in **holls athin waas** (holes in walls), **kyunnen holls** (rabbit holes) and in **roogs o stanes** (heaps of stones).

The **whaap** is a large brown bird, with a thin downward-curving **neb** (beak). If it sees you a long way off, it usually takes to the air, calling loudly. The **whaap** nests among the **seggy-flooers**, **cockiloories** and **smora** (yellow iris, daisies and clover). Most **whaaps** remain in Shetland during the winter but can leave if the weather turns nasty.

Whaap or **Spooi** *(Curlew)*. NH

Birds commonly seen in Shetland, in alphabetical order by Shetland name(s). Superscript numbers indicate that more than one Shetland name is listed for the bird.

Alamootie	Storm petrel
Baagie	Greater black-backed gull [1]
Banks sporrow (sparrow)	Rock pipit
Blackie	Blackbird
Bonxie	Great skua [1]
Chak	Wheatear [1]
Corbie	Raven
Dunter	Eider
Hegri	Heron
Horse-gock	Snipe [1]
Laverock	Lark
Lintie	Twite
Maa	Herring gull
Maalie	Fulmar
Peerie Whaap	Whimbrel [1]
Peewit	Lapwing [1]
Plivver	Golden plover
Rain-gös	Red-throated diver
Robbie Cuddie	Shetland wren
Saandiloo	Ringed plover
Shalder	Oystercatcher
Skarf	Cormorant or shag
Skooi	Great skua [2]
Skooty-alan/aalin	Arctic skua
Snippick	Snipe [2]
Snaa fool	Snow bunting
Solan	Gannet

Spooi	Curlew[1]
Staneshakker	Wheatear[2]
Stinkle	Wheatear[3]
Stirling	Starling
Swaabie	Greater black-backed gull [2]
Tang whaap	Whimbrel [2]
Tammie Norie	Puffin
Teetick	Meadow pipit
Tieve's Nacket	Lapwing [2]
Tirrick	Arctic tern
Tystie	Black guillemot
Whaap	Curlew[2]

NH

The Channerwick burn with
Levenwick beach in the distance. NH

60°N

Place-names

Discussion of place-name etymologies can be lengthy and is beyond the scope of this little dialect booklet. Many visitors to Shetland comment on the impression that they are no longer in Scotland but have moved to a Scandinavian country.

The selection of names given here focuses on those names which were created at some point during the period of some 800-900 years when the Scandinavian language known as Norn was spoken in Shetland, leaving its mark on the present dialect and place-names.

A sample of island names

Mousa

Many island names, like **Mousa**, now end with **-a** (sometimes **-ay** or **-y**) from Old Norse (ON) *öy* island.

A selection of other island names with this ending is: **Bressay**, **Burra**, **(Muckle) Flugga**, **Foula**, **Papa**, **Trondra**, **Vaila**, **Vementry** and **Whalsay**.

All photographs of road signs – DW

RM

Waiting in lane to cross on ferries to these islands creates an opportunity for photography and road sign collecting can become a happy holiday obsession!

Not all place-names ending in **-a** are island names and a degree of caution is required. One should take time to locate the island before deciding on the etymology of the name. Consider **Basta** and **Tresta** which are listed among the settlement names given later.

A small sample of names of settlements

Welcome to
AITH
Eið
(Old Norse: isthmus)

Very occasionally, as on the sign at **Aith** on the west side of Shetland (**Da Wastside**), an interpretation of a place-name is given on a road sign. This is informative for the walker who can pause to digest the information offered, but less safe for the passing driver.

There are many questions still to be answered, such as 'Where is the isthmus?' in this instance, or 'Where was the parliament/assembly place?' indicated in the following picture of the **Tingwall** road sign. Determined tourists will find it beside the loch lying to the south of the **Tingwall Kirk** (church).

Some of the road signs used here as illustrations of these coastal names may have been replaced or, indeed, the building to which they are attached may either have been repaired or fallen down, but it can be fun to collect the most idiosyncratic road sign possible and preserve it for posterity!

Many settlements are named after a prominent feature or aspect of the local landscape and, because most of the older settlements are located by the sea, these are often coastal features, such as **firth** (fjord), **voe** (long, narrow inlet), **wick** (bay), **ness** (headland) and so on, from the Norn words *fjörðr*, *vágr*, *vík* and *nes*, as in **Firth**, **Laxfirth**, **Voe**, **Dury Voe**, **Lerwick**, **Westerwick**, **Hermaness**, **Scatness**.

*Ura**firth**, Northmavine*

*Strom**firth** and White**ness***

*East **Ness**, Ollaberry*

*Scat**ness**, Dunross**ness***

*Grut**ness** and Ler**wick**, signs at Sumburgh airport*

Kingland, Ollaberry

Many of the settlement names which have stood the test of time, and some that have been created more recently using words which continued in use for many centuries, indicate that some kind of farming, whether cultivation of the land or grazing of animals, took place at the spot named. Names which end in **-bister** (ON *bólstaðr*), **-garth** (ON *garðr*), **-setter** (ON *setr* or *sætr*) or **-sta** (ON *staðir*) all point to agricultural activities and further terms, such as **-land** which can be either of Norn or Scottish English origin, could be added to this short list. A word of caution when you come across an apparently Scandinavian name such as **Jarlshof**; it was invented by Sir Walter Scott for his novel, *The Pirate*, which is an imaginary tale set in Shetland and first published in 1874.

Tresta is a place-name ending in **-a** but it does not belong with the island names. The split in the word is between **Tre-** and **sta**, with **-sta** being the modern form of ON *staðir* a farmstead. **Basta** is another example and there are others to be found on the map.

*Aith**setter** and Fladda**bister**,
Cunningsburgh*

*Culbins**garth** and Dandie**garth**,
Cunningsburgh*

The **Yell** sign below used to grace the waiting area for the ferry at Ulsta and it is sorely missed by at least one quirky photographer. It provided a splash of colour in a rather dull corner of the car park!

The name **Yell** departs from our theme of Scandinavian place-names in Shetland because it predates the Norn period and gives us a glimpse of what the earlier language might have been. The speakers have vanished from the place-name landscape, just as surely as this sign has vanished from the car park at Ulsta!

Some common Shetland Flowers

Banks Flooer *(Thrift or Sea-pink)* and **Grice Ingan** *(Spring Squill)*. MG

As the Shetland poet T.A. Robertson (Vagaland) memorably wrote at the start of his poem **'Shetlan Gairden'**:

> My gairden rins fir seeventy miles
> Fae Soombra Head ta Skaw …

Robertson, M (ed.), 1975. *Collected Poems of Vagaland*, The Shetland Times Ltd., p. 60.

Shetland's location on and above 60°N, along with its hilly topography and complex geology give rise to various habitats for wild **flooers**. The pink **banks flooers** and deep blue **grice ingans** can be seen from late May to late June/early July in rocky places where the **girse** (grass) is short, particularly by the coast, as in the photograph at Grutness (see page 27) in June. **Banks** is the word for coastal cliffs, or for a man-made 'cliff' as in the

paet bank which has been cut into the moor by a man or woman with a **tushkar** (implement for cutting peats). The drifts of pink **banks flooers** are real harbingers of summer. The name **grice murrick** refers not to the beautiful blue flower but to the plant's edible root which was grubbed up by **grice** (pigs). The runts of a crop of potatoes were also described as **murricks** and were fed to the omnivorous **grice**.

Hedder (Heather). DW

> **'Da hedder-ön is da very breath**
> **O da Sooth wind ower da hills.'**
> (The sultry scent of heather is the very breath
> Of the South wind over the hills.)

Robertson, T.A., (Vagaland), 'Hjalta' (You can listen to this poem on the *Shetland ForWirds* website).

Hedder grows in all upland parts of Shetland and often close to the coast as well and several different varieties can be distinguished. **Hedder** varies in colour from white (a less common plant, thought to be lucky) to the vivid purple seen on the **hill** (in the dialect sense of moorland which can have agricultural uses) in August. **Bell hedder**, with its beautiful rose-pink bell-shaped **flooers**, prefers better-drained ground, but it is a common plant. **Berry hedder** (crowberry) is also common but its shiny black berries can be difficult to find. **Bairns** (children) love searching for them among the bright green leaves of this variety of **hedder**, although the bitter taste of the berry is a little disappointing.

The green grass of re-seeded land can be seen in the photograph opposite, as in many parts of Shetland where crofters have been trying to improve their land.

Vagaland also wrote more than one poem about these vivid flowers (marsh-marigolds), which are called **blugga**.

As the English name 'marsh-marigold' suggests, **blugga** grows close to water and it is a common plant in most parts of Shetland.

*Below: **Blugga** (Marsh-marigold). BM*

Another plant which has a beautiful, but much smaller, yellow flower is **bark** (tormentil), with its **bark-flooer** seen here growing along with pink **honey-sookies** (lousewort), as is often the case because both are moorland plants. Children knew to suck on the sweet white stem of the **honey-sookie** to extract its delicate juice.

The root of the **bark** was far from sweet but it was favoured by **grice** (pigs) which grubbed up the nut-like root – hence the Scots name 'pig-nut' for English 'earth-nut'.

Bark (Tormentil) **and honey-sookies** (Lousewort). NH

Flowering plants commonly seen in Shetland, in alphabetical order by Shetland name. (Superscript numbers against entries in the second column indicate that more than one dialect name is listed for the flower and you will find the alternative(s) as you read through the list.)

Baldeerie	Heath spotted-orchid [1]
Banks-flooer	Thrift or Sea pink
Bark, bark-flooer	Tormentil
Blugga	Marsh-marigold
Clockie-flooer	Red campion [1]
Clowie-flooer	Bog asphodel [1]
Cock an da hen an da glyde-eyed shicken	Bird's-foot-trefoil [1]
Curldodie/Curl-dodie	Heath spotted-orchid [2]
Daa-nettle	Dead-nettle
Devil's mitten	Heath spotted-orchid [3]
Eksis girse	Hawkbit
Grice-murrick	Spring squill
Gulsa girse	Bogbean
Hedder	Heather
Honey-sookies	Lousewort
Johnsmas-flooer	Ribwort plantain
Kattiklu	Bird's-foot-trefoil [2]
Klonger	Dog rose
Kokkiloori/Kokkilurie	Daisy
Kokkilurie, Muckle	Ox-eye daisy
Kraatae	Creeping buttercup
Lammas flooer	Eyebright
Limrek	Bog asphodel [2]
Lukki's Oo	Cotton grass [1]
Luckaminnie's / Luckie-minnie's Oo	Cotton grass [2]
May-flooer	Primrose
Raggie Willie	Ragged-Robin
Runshie	Charlock, wild mustard
Segg, seggie-flooer	Yellow iris
Smora	White clover
Sweet William	Red campion [2]
Swittik	Wild angelica
Taegirse	Wild Thyme

Trowie cairds	Bracken, but commonly used for all ferns
Trowie gliv	Foxglove
White Kaitrins	Grass-of-Parnassus
Yölgirse	Meadowsweet

There are many ways of spelling the dialect name of the daisy, a common flower of the **mödoos** (meadows) and roadsides. It flourishes throughout **da simmer monts** (the summer months) and well into **da hairst** (the autumn). Its larger botanical cousin, called by some **Da Muckle Kokkilurie** (The Ox-eye Daisy), crops up in many places where **girse** predominates, such as **kirkyards** (churchyards) and **mödoos**.

Da Kokkiluri also features in a poem of that name.

Dey wir ee peerie white Kokkiluri
*   at grew*
At da side o da lodberry waa;
Hit wid open hits lips ta da moarnin
*   dew,*
An close dem at night whin da
*   caald wind blew,*
An rowe up hits frills in a peerie
*   roond clew*
As white as da flukkra snaa.

Angus, J.S., 1830-1923. Graham, J.J. & Graham, L.I. (eds.), 1998. *A Shetland Anthology*, Lerwick, p.22.

Kokkilurie / Kokkaloorie / Kokkalurie / Kockaloorie / Cockiloorie etc. (Daisy). NH

Cock an da hen an da glyde-eyed shicken (Cock and the Hen and the Squint-eyed Chicken), or **Kattiklu** (Cat's Claw), (Bird's-foot-trefoil). NH

Can you see the cock, hen and squint-eyed chicken in this bright yellow-orange **flooer**? Or perhaps it is easier to see the cat's claw? Or even the bird's foot of its English name, bird's-foot-trefoil?

This lovely **peerie** plant **flooers** in dry, grassy places from late May to August and adults can enjoy telling children about its various names as they walk along roads or by the coast.

The soft, tactile plant on the right is common on wet moorland, where the seed-heads make a splash of white in June/July. It flourishes on peaty ground.

Some people think that **Luckie** represents the name of the god, Loki, but this is by no means certain. **Minnie** is a word for 'grandmother' in the dialect, according to John Graham (*The Shetland Dictionary*), but the word is not in use now. Luckie-minnie or Lukka-minnie is a bad fairy in Shetland folk tales and it is thought, by some, to be unlucky to have this plant in the house, although it does look most attractive in a vase and lasts throughout the winter.

Lukki's Oo or Luckie-minnie's Oo. (Lukki's Wool), (Common Cotton-grass, Bog Cotton). NH

Curldodie (Heath Spotted-orchid). NH

The **curldodie** is a **flooer** which you will find tucked in among **da mödoo girse** (the meadow grass). It is a delicate pale lilac in colour and blossoms from late May to July. There are also darker purple variants of the spotted-orchid. The names **baldeerie** and **devil's mitten** are recorded as alternatives for **curldodie** by Rhoda Bulter (*Shetland Folk Book, IX,* p.15), although these names are not in common use. The Dictionary of the Older Scottish Tongue lists this as a name for the ribwort plantain but in Shetland the ribwort plantain is known as **Da Johnsmas-flooer** (see Scott, W. and Palmer, R., p. 274 for folklore associated with this plant in Scandinavia and the Northern Isles.)

Seggs are widespread in Shetland, often growing in large clumps on marshy land by streams. It is not loved nowadays by crofters whose fields it invades, although it was apparently not always so:

'The Seggey-flooer … dried in the August hay, makes a succulent and well-liked morsel for the peerie lambs in the winter.' *New Shetlander*, 1949, No.19, 27.

Bairns (children) use the spikey leaves of the **segg** to make toy **seggie boats** to sail in the **burns** (streams) beside which the plant most frequently grows.

Segg, Seggie-flooer (Yellow Iris). NH

DW

To make a **seggie boat**, choose one of the large pointed leaves of the **segg** and, having made a central slit towards the wide end of the leaf, insert the pointed end into this slit sideways, so that it holds firm and extends a little below the leaf to form a rudder. The looped leaf then acts like a sail and, when placed in the **burn**, the **seggie boat**, should drift with the flow of water. Have fun!

Food and Drink

Sassermaet. LJ

Maet (meat) is the generic dialect word for food.

Wid du laek a coarn o maet?:
Would you like some food?

Dunna glaep dy maet: Don't gobble your food

Faerdie maet: food to be eaten on a journey.

Sassermaet: spiced, minced meat, served with onions! (pictured above)

There have been many changes in eating habits in recent years, not least in the pattern of meals eaten in the day.

Traditional pattern of meals:

brakfast	breakfast
gruel	porridge
twal	morning tea/coffee break
bannocks klined wi butter an jam	scones spread with butter and jam
denner	main meal eaten at lunchtime
(mutton an taaties etc.)	
tae	high tea, maybe with **sassermaet**
eight o'clocks	tea, **bannocks**, cakes etc.
supper	cocoa/ovaltine etc. with a **baker's biscuit**

Recipes in recent cookery books reflect the international nature of food eaten in Shetland and many Shetlanders now have dinner in the evening rather than in the middle of the day, to suit changed working patterns. Some of the dialect words listed in this section are, therefore, no longer in regular use but Shetlanders still enjoy many of the seasonal dishes which were part of the diet of their forebears and they particularly enjoy engaging in the catching of their food.

Some kinds of baker's biscuits. LJ

Fysh (fish) and
shallfysh (shellfish)

Craigsaet: rock used as a seat
while fishing from the shore with
a **waand**

Gyaain ta da eela: going rod-
fishing in a small boat

Gyaain ta da troots: going to catch
trout, whether in sea or loch

**Gadderin spoots/wylks/lempits
etc.**: gathering razor clams/
whelks/limpets etc.

Da wylk ebb: the foreshore,
exposed at low tide, where
whelks can be gathered

fleuk, flook	flounder
hoe	piked dog-fish
lempit	limpet (used for bait)
masgoom	monkfish
olick	young ling
piltick / piltock	coalfish, two to four years old
raan	roe of a fish
said	saithe (full grown coalfish)
sillick / sillock	young saithe
skeetik	squid
spoot	razor-clam
stenbiter	catfish
troot	trout
wylk	whelk
yoag	large horse-mussel

Some of the other fish and shellfish
which are regularly eaten are
referred to by the English name for
the species: cod, crab, haddock,
hake, halibut, herring, ling, lobster,
mackerel (pronounced **machrel** by
some), monkfish (often just **monk**
rather than **masgoom**), mussels,
plaice, salmon, scallops, sole,
whiting.

Some ways of preparing fish for eating

Krappin: mixture of finely chopped fish livers, flour, oatmeal and seasoning, traditionally used to stuff the head of the fish which is then boiled until cooked. At the **Voe Eela** Competition it is sometimes cooked and served up in a **kale bled** (cabbage leaf) – another traditional method. Greaseproof paper or a boil-in-the-bag will do.

Potted herring and mackerel: mackerel baked slowly in equal parts vinegar and water is particularly delicious and still popular in the mackerel season.

Saat piltick (salted coalfish): these salt fish used to be a common sight hanging on ropes at the sides of croft houses to dry. Refrigeration has removed the need to preserve fish in this way, although some **pilticks** can still be seen **hingin on a raep** (hanging on a rope) on the **gavel** (gable) of houses. Salt cod and ling can still be bought in fish shops because they are commercially produced but it is not easy to buy **pilticks**.

'Wir Frank' hingin oot pilticks
(Frank Manson hanging out salted
pilticks to dry in the wind). MB

Mark Fullerton an Lindsay Angus enjoyin monk tails an scallops i da hold o da boat. CS

They were on a fishing research trip, which clearly had its culinary attractions as they sampled monkfish and scallops in 'a brilliant chowder', as Charlie Simpson said.

Sookit pilticks: dried by exposure to the wind and boiled before eating.

Stap: a dish in which the cooked liver and soft parts of the head of a fish are mixed together, then seasoned. This is infrequently eaten nowadays but some people do enjoy it for supper after being **at da eela**.

Flesh (meat)

Lamb is, of course, the meat that Shetland is famous for around the world. It is prepared in all the usual ways but there is also **reestit mutton,** which is a method of further preserving heavily salted meat by hanging it in the roof of a croft-house kitchen and allowing it to become smoke-dried. It is regarded as a delicacy and is eaten along with potato soup (**reestit mutton and taatie soup**), usually served along with **bannocks** made with white flour. This is popular fare in the halls which are open overnight at **Up Helly Aa** when hungry guizers expect traditional food.

*Bab and Jack wi twartree reestit tees (Bab and Jack Fraser with some **reestit legs of lamb** hanging up to dry). IS*

More archaic than **reestit mutton** was **vivda**, which was mutton dried without salt in a **skeo** – a hut for storing and wind-drying fish or meat, so constructed that the wind passed freely through the stones.

Also traditional are **puddens** or **puddings** (in which the **u** in the first syllable is pronounced like the **u** in English cup). These are made from the intestines of sheep and can be made with dried fruit (**curny puddings**) or oatmeal (**aetmel puddings**) or the lamb's liver (**liver puddings**).

Beef is also eaten in all the usual forms and preparations, but **sassermaet**, illustrated at the start of the section, is a specifically Shetland recipe for dealing with the poorer cuts of minced beef. It is similar to Lorne Sausage but much more highly spiced and is served fried in the shape of a **brönnie** (round, thick oatmeal scone).

Twa curny puddings, or is it wan big een, juist waitin ta be aeten!
(Two fruit puddings, or is it one big one, just waiting to be eaten!). CS

Some other dialect words (or dialect ways of pronouncing English words) for food and liquid accompaniments are listed below:

blaand	sour whey
brö	the water in which any kind of food has been boiled (e.g. **mutton brö**)
shicken	chicken
deuk	duck
gös	goose
kale, kel	cabbage
kirn; kirn mylk	churn; **kirn mylk** is a solid product resembling cottage cheese in structure
mellie taaties	floury potatoes, much prized
myl-gruel	porridge made with milk instead of water
mylk (**my** in **mylk** pronounced as English 'my')	milk
neep	turnip
saat	salt
tee o mutton	leg of mutton

A fine kel hert ta pit ida mutton brö
(A fine cabbage heart to putin the mutton broth). LS

Bread and baking

The proliferation of Sunday Teas in local halls throughout Shetland has boosted local baking as women produce astonishing numbers of **tabnabs** (home-baked pastries or cakes) to tempt the palates of locals and visitors alike. **Tabnab** is not really a dialect word but it is thought to have originated in the Merchant Navy and is popular with workers on the North Sea oil rigs.

People seeing a plate of **tabnabs** might well say they are **fantin/ black fantin** (very hungry indeed)! The tea served along with the **tabnabs** should be piping hot, not **loo** (lukewarm) and at the end one is likely to be absolutely **foo** (full) or **stentit** (stomach stretched to bursting point)!

Children express approval of taste by saying **'Nyim, nyim!'** and the opposite would be **'Gadge!'**

Bannocks klined wi butter an jam (Bannocks spread with butter and jam). IJ

baker's biscuit	large, plain biscuits made and sold by bakers in Shetland
bannock	scone made with white flour
beremel bannock	scone made with beremeal flour
brönnie	round, thick oatmeal scone
brunt	burnt (seldom!)
flooer	flour
huffsi	fruit loaf
loff	loaf of bread
raem	cream, to serve with jam on occasion
rhuburb	rhubarb (Shetland's principal jam)
saat	salt
shilpit (adj.)	tart and **soor** (sour) in taste
shuggar	sugar
sturken (v)	harden, like fat as it cools
tristy	thirsty and in need of a drink

A hamper o goodies. KM

Favourite Words

NOUNS

aamos	gift promised in the hope that it will bring good luck to the donor
aert	earth
aestard	an easterly direction
bairn	child
banks	coastal cliffs
ben	best room in a cottage, for visitors
bruck	rubbish
but	kitchen-cum-living room, for everyday use
caa	a drive of sheep or, in the past, whales
calloo	long-tailed duck
crub	small, circular stone enclosure
damoarn / da moarn	tomorrow
dastreen / da streen	yesterday evening
dayset	nightfall, dusk
dimriv	dawn
ee(n)	eye(s)
essy-kert	bin lorry
feerie	bug or illness of some kind
forsmo	insult, shocking surprise
foy	party
gansey	thick jumper
gluff	fright
guddick	riddle
hooroo	uproar
hoose	house

host	cough
ime	soot formed on the outside of a cooking pot
jookerie-packerie	trickery
kabbilabbi	the sound of many people speaking at the same time
kirk	church
kirn	churn
kishie	straw basket carried on the back
krö / crö	pen for sheep
lipper	nasty person
lock	great deal
mirknen	evening twilight, late twilight
Mirry-dancers	Aurora Borealis
möld	earth
neesick	porpoise
noost	place where rowing boat is drawn up out of the sea
ormal	tiny particle, scrap
paddock-stöl	mushroom
quoy	piece of common land enclosed and cultivated (place-name)
roog	round heap (of peats, for example)
scaar	small amount
shoormal	high water mark on the beach; the water's edge
skorie	young herring gull
skurt	bosom, within folded arms
slester	gooey mess
smoorikin	kiss
smucks	slippers

spaegie	muscle pain
start	short period of time
trooker	naughty person
trow	one of the 'little people' of Shetland
udal	ancient Scandinavian system of land tenure
Up-Helly-Aa	fire festival, held on last Tuesday in January in Lerwick
uplowsin	thaw caused by heavy rain; a deluge of rain
vaelensi	very stormy weather
vynd	a style or way of doing something
waageng	unpleasant taste (or smell) which lingers
yackle	molar tooth
yowe	female sheep
Zetland	old county name for Shetland

PRONOUNS

du, dee, dy, dine	you, your, yours (singular, familiar)
shö	she
hit, hits	it, its
we, wir, wirs	we, our, ours
dey, der, ders	they, their, theirs
dis, dat, yun	this, that, that over there

ADJECTIVES

aert-kent	known very widely
aald	old
blyde	glad

caald, cowld	cold
disjaskit	exhausted, worn out
dorty	sulky
eident	hard-working
filskit, filsket	high-spirited, frisky
glowerit	lurid
halliget	wild, given to unrestrained behaviour
ill-best	best available, best of a poor bunch
ill-laek	not good looking
ill-vyndit	clumsy or awkward in action
lang	long
lightsome	cheerful and cheering
moaderate	even-tempered, quiet and unassuming (person)
muckle	big
nipsiccar	caustic in manner
obstropolous	difficult to control
overly	over-the-top, excessive
peerie	small
perskeet	prim
pöraamos	not very strong, frail
raamished	peevish through lack of sleep
shilpit	sour-tasting
stoot	fat, stout
tirn	bad-tempered, angry
twartree	two or three, a few
unkan	unfamiliar, from another place
uploppm	boisterous
veeve	vivid, easy to see
vexed	sorry, disappointed

| wenglit | gangly |
| yasp | energetic |

VERBS

aandoo	row gently against the tide in order to maintain a boat's position
ant	heed or pay attention to
bröl	bellow; to make a loud mooing noise, like a cow
buks	walk or trudge heavily, as through snow
crex	clear the throat
cummel	turn upside down
dort	sulk
dwaam	faint or go into a semi-conscious state, unaware of surroundings
ebb	go out, applying to the tide
froad	froth, usually at the mouth with anger
gowl	cry loudly
hurl	push along, as of a wheelbarrow
igg	incite, usually 'igg on'
keek	peep
knap	speak English, used of Shetland dialect speakers
leet	heed
lippen	expect
miscaa	speak ill of
murn	weep
neester	creak or squeak
nyaarg	nag

oag	crawl
owse	bale out water, as from a boat
peester	squeak, squeal
proag	poke around
rive	tear
roo	pluck the wool off a sheep

SIMILES

as black as da paet	as black as the peat, very black indeed
as clean as a preen	as clean as a pin, very clean indeed
as fat as a neesik/neesick	as fat as a harbour porpoise
as fat as (s)he can lie ida hide	as fat as the person's skin can hold without splitting
as lang as da day an da moarn	as long as today and tomorrow put together
as waik as wal watter	as weak as water drawn from a well (no strong spirits here!)

IDIOMATIC EXPRESSIONS

At da aidge o a time	Occasionally
Come dee wiz	Come along with me
Mak a lang airm	Help yourself to food at the table
Never spaek	No need to say anything; all is clear to the listener
Peety aboot dee	Serve you right
Tak du on	Whine as much as you want. No sympathy will be forthcoming
Tak dy fit i dy haand	Let's get walking

Sea & Boats

Shetlanders love **da sea** and have many words relating to it in all its moods.

Da Rigg, Dale o Waas, an elongated headland by the Voe of Dale, with sea foaming against the rocky coastline. This **shore brak** (break), as it is known, is a common sight along the coastline of Shetland. *Da Rigg* (literally 'ridge') is also used of the human spine. DW

*Another splendid example of **shore brak**. KM*

***Selkies** relaxing on the rocks. KM*

Banks, stacks and skerries at Braewick, Eshaness. JC

Shetland
ForWirds

Kirk Holm, off the point of Kirkaness, Sand. JC

*A **geo** with the island of **Foula** on the horizon. JC*

Words referring to the sea and coast:

affrug	reflux of waves after having broken on the shore
ayre	shingly beach
baa	sunken rock, exposed at low tide
banks broo	edge of the cliffs (see p.58)
brennastyooch (sometimes **brimmasteuch**)	fine spray rising from sea breaking on the rocky shore
brimtud	sound of sea breaking on the shore
drongs	pointed rocks in the sea – as in the photograph of **Da Drongs** (see p.54)
ebb	foreshore, exposed at low tide
fram	seawards, out to sea
geo, gyo	small, steep, precipitous inlet (see p.56)
haaf	open sea
holm	small isle not far from shore
houb	a lagoon (see p.58)
laebrak	surf, long wave breaking on the shore
lönabrak	swell and surge of sea breaking on the shore
meid	prominent feature on the land which, when lined up with another landmark, enables fishermen to establish and maintain their position at sea

Left: **Banks broo**. JC

Below: **Da houb** at Kirk
Ness, Brough, Whalsay. JC

moder dy	landward-tending swell of the sea, which experienced **haaf-fishermen** could detect and use as a guide to land
roost (Da Roost)	tide race (local name for the rough stretch of water to the south of Sumburgh Head)
saatbrak	sea spray
shoormal	highwater mark on the beach; the water's edge
skerry	rock in the sea
stack	high, prominent rock in the sea
vaddel	sea-pool at the head of a **voe** which fills and empties with the tide
voe	inlet of the sea, generally long and narrow
wick	bay, generally broader than a **voe**

Many of these dialect words for coastal features can be spotted in place-names, such as Gulberwick, Rerwick, Sandwick, Westerwick etc. Gulberwick derives from Old Norse *Gullberuvík*, from the female personal name *Gullbera*. You should see if you can find further examples on road signs as you drive or cycle around Shetland.

Words referring to the use of boats:

aer	oar
aandoo	row gently against the tide in order to maintain a boat's position
böd	fisherman's hut
dorro	handline with several hooked lines attached, used in catching mackerel, **piltocks** (coalfish) etc
fourareen	four-oared boat
hinnyspot	three-cornered piece of wood connecting the gunwales of a boat with the stem
lodberrie	type of 18th-century house in Lerwick, built with its foundations in the sea, and combining pier, courtyard, store and dwelling-house
noost/noust	sheltered place where a boat can be drawn up to protect it from the sea; usually excavated from the **banks**
owskerri	scoop for bailing water out of a boat
shoo	row a boat stern foremost by backing with the oars
sixern, sixareen	six-oared boat
tafts	seats in a traditional boat
tilfers	boat floorboards
tully	large open knife with a wooden handle, used by fishermen for splitting fish
waand	fishing rod
yoal	six-oared boat, slimmer and smaller than a sixern; widely used in rowing races

*The door of a **lodberrie** in Lerwick, NH*

The same yoal design once used to pursue the fishing for a living is now used mainly for pleasure. This photograph was taken at one of Shetland's many popular summertime rowing regattas and features a Bigton team. NS

Above: Yoal race. NS
Below: Shetland Model sailing boats getting ready for a race at the annual Inter-club Regatta in Lerwick. KM

Fiddles & Music

Dr Tom Anderson.

Shetland is world-renowned for its fiddle music and the tradition is still very much alive.

One of Shetland's best known 20th century fiddlers was Tom Anderson (1910-91) or Tammie Anderson as he was generally known at **hame**. As a teacher, composer and collector his influence on Shetland music has been inspirational and far-reaching. A group of fiddlers he assembled for the 1960 **Hamefarin** became the Shetland Fiddlers Society who practise weekly. He initiated Shetland fiddle music tuition in the schools in the 1970s and many of today's fiddle instructors are former pupils. Among them are members of the group who were originally dubbed **Tammie's Peerie Angels**. Grown up now, they are known as **Shetland's Heritage Fiddlers**.

The names of some of the tunes Tammie collected and composed are a rich source of dialect words, often incorporating the place-names which were important in the various stages of Tammie's life from his childhood in Eshaness onwards.

Some of Tammie's tune names will be the focus here, so '**Haand me doon da fiddle**', '**Gie's an A**' an **let's get goin**! (Hand me down the fiddle, give us an A (to start the tuning process) and let's get going).

Above: Shetland's Heritage Fiddlers. DS

*Left: Callum Watt, Walls. Callum was
Young Fiddler of the Year 2013. DC*

The following selection is random,
chosen solely to illustrate the use
of dialect in the naming of tunes.
Traditional tunes are marked (trad.)
to distinguish them from Tammie's
own compositions.

Slow airs or melodies

(Da) Auld Planti Crü	(The) old stone enclosure for protecting plants while they grow. They were generally sited on land outside the **hill daeks**
(Da) Auld Restin Chair (one of Tammie's best-known tunes)	Old wooden seat of a type commonly seen in croft houses in the past – a long seat with back and arms – theoretically for resting in, but not very soft!
Broch o Hamnavoe	Brochs seemed to inspire music, this one is in Hamnavoe, Eshaness, near where Tammie grew up
(Da) Cryin Taing	Point of land at Ronas Voe from which people could call to someone on the other side, often calling for a boat to transport them across the water. **Kalliness** in Whiteness/Weisdale has the same meaning

*Thanks to Ian Tait, Curator, Shetland Museum and Archives, for this splendid picture of a **krobb**, **crub** or **crü** (above), as it is written in the name of Tammie's tune **Da Auld Planti Crü**.*

Daybrak	Daybreak or dawn
Dunters ida Voe	Eider ducks in the **voe** (inlet of the sea)
Fine Hairst Mornin	Fine harvest morning
(Da) Lonely Smisslen	Lonely sand-gaper shellfish
(Da) Mousa Broch	See comment about **Broch o Hamnavoe**
Pund Head	Headland in Hamnavoe, Eshaness with an enclosure where animals could be gathered
Shoormal	The water's edge on a beach (see p.59)
(Da) Slockit Light	Extinguished light – probably his best known melody – marking both the passing of people and of a way of life
(Da) Troublesome Tivlick	Troublesome joint, as in the spine

The range of life experience covered in the names of tunes composed or collected by Tammie is both surprising and amusing, as in **Da Troublesome Tivlick**. Music was a constant part of his mental landscape, whether slow airs or faster reels, hornpipes and jigs. He used the physical world to convey his imaginative inner world to his listeners. Like many fiddlers he liked to use places and people in his tune names.

Aly's Soond	A tribute from Tammie to a young master of traditional fiddle music – Aly Bain
Bekka Hill	A hill in Sand, opposite the village of Garderhouse where Tammie's wife grew up.

(Da) Boannie Isle o Whalsa (trad.)	Beautiful island of Whalsay
(Da) Brakkin Baa	Sunken rock in the sea over which the sea would regularly break; the words and the music work together to create the sound of the sea.
Eshaness Two Step	Written to accompany the popular dance, the Boston Two Step
Lament for Lowrie ida Lea	Tammie often used alliteration to give a musical quality to the words in the name of a tune, as in this lament for a friend, **Lowrie (who lived) in the Lea**.
Oot be Aest Da Vong (trad.)	To the East of the Vong. A traditional tune played in Vidlin to accompany the dance known as **Da Shetlan Reel** (The Shetland Reel). **Da Vong** is a large rock between Whalsay and Skerries.
(Da) Selkie Stane	Seal Stone, a rock beside the sea in Eshaness, from which Tammie learned to dive as a child.
(Da) Shaalds o Foula (trad.)	A very old tune which accompanied the dance known as **Da Foula Reel**. **Da Shaalds** are hidden reefs at the north end of Foula.
Shalder Geo (trad.)	Oystercatcher geo (see page 56 for photograph of a **geo**).
Shingly Beach	This is the beach at Stenness, Eshaness, where agates can be found among the stones (by the sharpsighted).

(Da) Trowie Burn (Freedaman Stickle)	A burn associated with **da trows**, Shetland's little folk, often **ill-tricket**, sometimes malicious, who were constantly tempting fiddlers to join them. This tune is credited to a legendary Unst fiddler.
Violet Tulloch's Hornpipe	A tribute to Tammie's able accompanist on piano.
(Da) Craw Dang Pussy (trad.)	A game in which a tame crow knocked the cat over. This has been chosen as the name of a modern group.

Three of Shetland's most revered musicians, Peerie Willie Johnson (1920-2007), Violet Tulloch and Aly Bain.

Aandooin at da bow (trad.)	Rowing gently against the movement of the water when at sea in order to keep the boat in a particular spot.
Aald Swaara (trad.)	**Swaara** was a thick, heavy yarn often used for knitting workclothes and undergarments. The fisherman's **joopie** (a woollen shirt or singlet) was knitted in dark wool. According to Peter Fraser this tune was composed in deep sorrow as a lament for fishermen lost at sea during the haaf fishing.
Deil Stick da Minister (trad.)	Not a popular gentleman, this minister! Originally a Scottish tune written after an attempt by the Church of Scotland to ban dancing.

Mak a Kishie Needle, Dye (trad.)

A **kishie** was the straw basket carried on the back and this tune asks **Dye** (grandfather) to make the wooden needle which was used in making **kishies**. It is a tune for a traditional reel and was collected from Peter Fraser on **Da Wastside**.

Right: A kishie, see above. DC

*Below: **Aertkent** band Fiddlers' Bid whose lively contemporary style is firmly rooted in Shetland's traditional music.*

Sandwick with HIllswick
Ness and Da Drongs in the
distance. NH

The Weather

Da wadder (the weather) is a very frequent topic of conversation in Shetland where it is no exaggeration to say that aspects of all four seasons can be experienced in a week, or even in a day!

voar (spring) – da **saandiloos** (ringed plovers) are come

simmer (simmer) – **Johnsmas** (24 June) **flooers** are in bloom

hairst (autumn) – **hairst blinks:** flashes of harvest lightning

winter: there is no special dialect word for winter, although pronunciation can identify the native Shetlander

A dryin wind in November is makkin a bed for snaa!: A good drying wind in November is just preparing for severe weather to come.

Sunsheen an snaale shooers ower Fitful.
(Sunshine and snowy showers over Fitful Head). DW

Wadder wirds an expressions (weather words and expressions)

bright, calm, fine, rainy, still, sunny, windy – as in English

wadder-head – pattern of clouds running in columns or streaks across the sky, traditionally used in forecasting weather

Weather prediction was and is very important to the Shetlander. **Da Borrowin Days** are still remembered – these are the last three days of March and are supposed to be indicators of the weather for May, June and July respectively.

caald/cowld – cold
haet (1) – hot, e.g. a haet day
haet (2) – heat, e.g. I canna bear da haet

guid wadder – good weather
ill/coorse wadder – bad weather
day atween wadders – fine day between spells of poor weather
day o dirt – day of poor weather, usually rain
day o distress – day of rain and wind, worse than the above

Caald/cowld

a bittersie – a very cold day
pinnishin – suffering from extreme cold
stirn – shiver with the cold
stivven – become stiff with cold

Haet

close – close (adj.), hot and airless
leepin wi haet – feeling very hot (par-boiling!)

*Below: What weather would **you** expect to follow from **a wadder-head** like this? BM*

Caption reads: **"An ta tink we micht hae büne sookin apo a bit o suggar i' Buckingham Palace!"** *(After the Royal visit when the Queen was presented with a Shetland pony in Unst). Reprinted from F. S. Walterson & J Tait Island Laughter, with kind permission of the Walterson family.*

simmer blink – a short blink of sunshine promising, but not delivering, heat

simmer mirr/simmermal dance – shimmering of the air on a hot day

Mist

daalamist – mist which gathers in valleys at night

ask – mist

barber, frosty barber – freezing mist drifting over the sea

dag – thick mist/light drizzle

steekit mist – very thick mist

'If du sees fog on da hill in January, hit'll edder blaa awa or snaa awa': January fog on the hill is not a sign of good weather to come.

Daalamist. NH

Da Broch at Clickhimin, Lerwick, in da snaa. KM

Snaa (snow)

bear – to drift, as snow driven by wind

fann – snowdrift

flukra – snow falling gently in large flakes

freezin laek da bon/bonfrost – freezing very hard indeed, like bone

glerl o ice – smooth glaze of ice on a surface (road, path etc.)

haily puckles – hailstones

moorie (moor-caavie) – blizzard (*blinnd* **moorie** – emphasises how thick and blinding the blizzard is)

towe – thaw

da towe is comin da moarn – the thaw is coming tomorrow

da snaa took aff – it stopped snowing

'If da snaa faas on 3rd January, da rain'll never melt it!' The snow which falls in early January will persist.

'If Candlemas Day (2 Feb.) be bright an fair
Half o da winter's ta come an mair
But if Candlemas Day be dark an dull
Half o da winter was dön at Yöl.'

Weet

doontöm – downpour

drush/droosh – drizzle

shooer – shower

Lammas speets – heavy showers in August (Lammas is 1 Aug.)

thunder speet – heavy rain along with thunder

vaanloop – downpour

vaelensi – downpour with violent gale, very stormy weather

hit's spittin a grain – there are a few raindrops

hit's laid on ta rain – it has begun to rain quite heavily, implying that it will continue for some time

hit's lowsed ta rain – it has begun to rain very heavily

hit's poorin/ tömin/a tömalt – it's pouring

hit's staandin aff o da aert – it's raining so hard the drops are bouncing off **da aert** the earth

we got sokkit/drookled/laid ta da hide – we got very wet indeed!

A plump o rain ta da suddert (a heavy rainstorm to the south). BM

Wind

Wind is the most common topic of weather-related conversation, for good reason!

dill awa – die down (as of wind)

ert – wind direction. (Very important to sailors: *'What's da ert o da wind da day?'*; *'What ert is he?'*)

flan – gust of wind

flyin gale – a strong gale-force wind

goosel/gooster – an unsteady, gusty wind

laar/pirr o wind – breath of wind, a very light wind

ree – spell of stormy weather

snitter – biting cold wind

he's makkin a guid drocht – it's a good drying day (for washing, **a guid sook** – drying peats, etc.)

da wind fell awa – the wind died down

da wind took up – the wind grew stronger

da wind guid aboot – the wind direction changed

Is da wind gyaain ta tak up or faa awa? What tink you?
(*Is the wind going to increase or decrease in strength? What do **you** think?*). BM

gaa – parhelion, mock sun,
   regarded as a portent of bad
   weather. A 'gaa afore da sun' is
   more to be feared.

A traditional rhyme runs as follows:

'A gaa afore, we'll hae a snore (of wind)
A gaa behind, we needna mind.'

Gaa ahint da sun. BM

This is a splendid example of a pure-bred Shetland ram with horns fully developed for **bultin** (butting). He looks very placid in this photograph but that may be deceptive. KM

Sheep & Knitting

There are many dialect words for Shetland sheep, their **oo** (wool) and the **makkin** (knitting) which some Shetland women still do by hand with **wirsit** (spun wool), although many of the garments which are on sale in shops are now made by machine. **Spinnin** (spinning) and **waevin** (weaving) were more common in the past than they are now, although the Shetland Guild of Spinners, Knitters, Weavers and Dyers work hard to preserve and promote the skills. Their 2012 book *A Legacy of Shetland Lace* includes a glossary of Shetland words associated with **makkin**.

DW

The soft, natural wool of Shetland sheep is prized. The **moorit** (reddish-brown) of the sheep in the foreground of this picture is particularly well known. The darker colour of the sheep in the background is known as **Shetland black** and people like it because it is not too starkly black.

Above: **Shaela-coloured Shetland yowes**. NS. Left: Sheep in **da crö/krö** (sheep-pen), probably waiting to be **clippit** (clipped) or **rooed** (have wool plucked off, in the case of native Shetland sheep). NH

NH

Twartree wirds ta dö wi sheep an der oo

(a few words to do with sheep and their wool)

almark	sheep which jumps over or through fences to escape
bjoag, branks, yoke	wooden triangle placed round the neck of the sheep to discourage attempts at escape
caa, caain	a drive of sheep, driving sheep
caddie, caddy	bottle-fed lamb which has lost its mother
catmoagit	of colour, light above and dark below
crö (krö)	sheep-pen
gimmer	female sheep before it has a lamb
greemit	of colour, dark marks on the face or legs
gulmoagit	of colour, dark above and light below
hentilagets, hent	tufts of wool fallen off sheep as they graze and then gathered or **hented**
moorit	reddish-brown colour of wool
nyaarmin	bleating
oo	wool
roo	pluck the wool off sheep
shaela	grey
sholmet	of colour, dark body and white face
yowe	ewe

This is a model of an old spinning wheel, now being used by a member of the Guild. Her husband made it. Hand-spinning has certainly seen a revival over the last couple of decades and we hope that will continue.

> Dat wis what she wanted, folk,
> Ta keep da life atil her –
> A grain o **oo** ta **caird** an spin
> An **mak** an sell for siller

Robertson, T.A. (Vagaland), 'Hae ye ony moorit oo?'
Robertson, M (ed.), 1975. *Collected Poems of Vagaland*, The Shetland Times Ltd., p. 65.

Twartree wirds ta dö wi spinnin an makkin

(a few words to do with spinning and knitting)

allover	jumper with an all-over Fair Isle pattern
caird	instrument for carding wool or, as a verb, to card wool
clew/cloo	ball of yarn
flee	flyer of spinning wheel
gansey	jersey
gra(a)vit	scarf
hank*	skein of yarn
hap	shawl
head*	4 **hanks** of yarn
hesp tree/reel	niddynoddy
mak, makkin, makkin belt	knit, knitting, leather belt used by some knitters to stabilise knitting needle
pirn/pirm	bobbin
rower	rolag/rollag, i.e. wool rolled between **cairds** in preparation for spinning
sock	any piece of knitting
spencer	waist-length woollen vest with V-neck
swaara	heavy, thick woollen yarn (see page 70)
sweerie-box	box for holding bobbins of yarn
sweerie-geng	first row in any piece of knitting
toorie	knitted hat, perhaps with pompom
waptree	rod connecting treadle to axle of spinning wheel
wires, wairs	knitting needles
wirsit	woollen yarn

* Note for those who wish to buy yarn. It is no longer sold in **hanks** and **heads**.

Makkin (knitting)

Shetland doesn't have a special word for knitting; to knit is to **mak** (make). **Makkin** skills developed out of necessity. Girls were not allowed to sit **haand-idle** (doing nothing). Trading hand-knitted goods to merchants was vital to the income of local families in the past. In hard times, it is no exaggeration to say that Shetland women knitted to survive.

> Whin times wis hard ida days afore wis
> Da folk wis wint ta **roo** an **hent**,
> Mak socks an sell dem ta da Dutchies,
> An dat wis da wye dey peyed da rent.

Robertson, T.A. (Vagaland), 'Minnie Spaeks', *Collected Poems*, p. 51.

The earliest knitted items for sale were stockings. Perhaps that's why the word for a piece of knitting – any piece of knitting – was, and still is, a **sock**. *'Tak dee sock, lass!'* means 'Take your knitting, girl!'

*Left: These **lightsome** (bright and cheerful) socks were worthy prizewinners in a Guild competition.*

From the 1930s onwards, machine-knitting became common practice, often in small factories. Garments were still finished by hand and hand-knitting of patterned garments continued. In the 1960s/70s many women, and some men, made a living from a **makkin-machine** at home. Machines became capable of knitting Fair Isle, later even **openwark** (lace patterns) though no machine could knit **fine lace** (one-ply, the finest weight). The knitwear industry was never so active again after the oil construction boom in the late 1970s. Hand-knitting too came to be much less prevalent, which is regrettable because:

> Your mind haes a joy o creation
> Laek writin a rhyme – hit's nae lee –
> Whin your fingers an **wires** in relation
> Maks da colours an patterns agree!

Stella Sutherland, 'Da allover', *A Celebration*, p. 23.

Below: This is an example of designers moving with the times and creating a **Fair Isle hoodie-allover** *(allover Fair Isle jumper with a hood).*

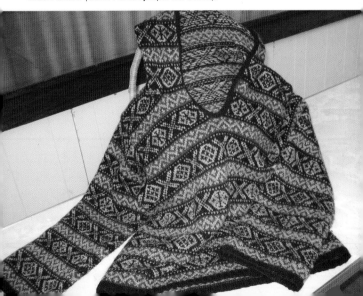

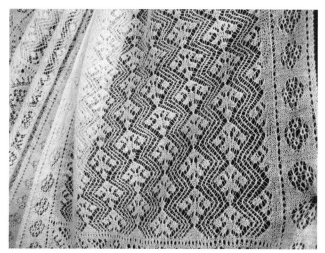

*Above: The delicacy of **openwark** (lace patterns) requires real skill, demonstrated here in this beautiful stole made by Sue Arthur.*

*Left: **Da makkin belt** (the knitting belt) has been used as a support for **wires** (knitting needles) for a very long time.*

(Unattributed photographs in this section by LJ and DW)

*Two beautiful Fair Isle fishermen's **keps**. AS*

A **spencer** – a long-sleeved,
waist-length woollen garment
reputedly named after George,
2nd Earl Spencer (1758-1834) –
worn originally as a man's jacket
over a **taily cot** (a long-tailed
coat). During the last century it
was used by many Shetlanders
as an undergarment to help keep
them warm in cold, wintry weather,
at whatever time of the year!
Sleeveless **spencers** have recently
enjoyed a rebirth in the fashion
world. *(This **spencer** (right) was
made by Zena Thomson.)*

A swatch o colours

(This is the sample card for all the Shetland wool colours sold at Jamieson & Smith, North Road, Lerwick, with some examples of Shetland dialect names for colours recorded at the side.)

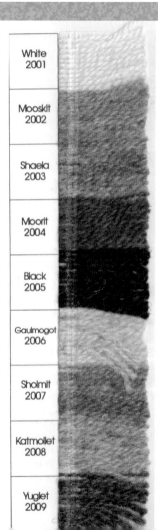

White	2001
Mooskit	2002
Shaela	2003
Moorit	2004
Black	2005
Gaulmogot	2006
Sholmit	2007
Katmollet	2008
Yuglet	2009

Up Helly Aa

For many Shetlanders this festival is the highlight of the year. It has some features which relate to Shetland`s Viking past, but originated only in the second half of the 19th century and has a carnival atmosphere.

On the last Tuesday in January, the replica of a Viking galley is dragged through the streets of Lerwick accompanied by 40-50 **squads** (groups) of **guizers** (men in costume) carrying burning torches. The leading guizer is the **Guizer Jarl**, and he and his squad are dressed as Vikings. The climax of the procession is the ceremonial burning in a central park when the guizers throw their torches onto the galley.

The Guizer Jarl's Squad of 2013 with the galley. KS

Above: The Up Helly Aa procession in full swing, 2006. KM
*Below: **Lang lippened, come at last!** (Long expected, here at last) The Lerwick Guizer Jarl has been waiting for 15 years for his day to come. KM*

Da lowin galley (The burning galley). KM

After the galley has been consumed in fire the various squads begin to visit in turn about 12 halls throughout Lerwick. In each hall they perform for the guests an act which may depict an event from contemporary Shetland life, some national or international occurrence or even a TV show or advert. The content of the act is often comical or satirical.

Festivities begin at 7.30pm and finish about 8am next morning. Lerwick Up Helly Aa is the main festival, but other similar festivals now take place throughout Shetland on a smaller scale: in Scalloway, Bressay, Nesting and Girlsta, Northmavine, Cullivoe, Uyeasound, the South Mainland, Delting and Norwick. In the rural festivals, women can be guizers too.

A lightsome night ida haal. Wan o da squads. Garden gnomes entertaining some of the guests at one of the 12 halls. KM

Acknowledgements

We are very grateful to all the photographers whose work plays such an important part in this book.

Mary Blance – *MB*.

Davy Cooper – *DM*.

John Coutts – *JC*.

Margaret Grønneberg – *MG*.

Nat Hall – *NH*.

Isobel Johnson – *IJ*.

Laureen Johnson – *LJ*.

Bill Moore – *BM*.

Keith Morrison – *KM*.

Robin Mouatt – *RM*.

Iris Sandison – *IS*.

Kenneth Shearer – *KS*.

Charlie Simpson – *CS*.

Anne Sinclair – *AS*.

Lise Sinclair – *LS*.

Nicola Sinclair – *NS*.

Dale Smith – *DS*.

Ian Tait – *IT*.

Doreen Waugh – *DW*.

The photograph of Dr Tom Anderson on p.64 was provided through the Scottish Traditional Music Hall of Fame website. Thank you to Simon Thoumire and Louis De Carlo for permission to use it.

The photograph on p.69 was provided courtesy of Violet Tulloch.

The photograph of Fiddlers' Bid on pp.70-71 was provided courtesy of Fiddlers' Bid.

The cartoon on p.75 was provided courtesy of the Walterson family.

We would also like to thank Charlie Simpson for his help with compiling the Fiddles and Music section.

References

Anderson, Dr Tom, 1986. *Haand Me Doon Da Fiddle*. Shetland Musical Heritage Trust.

Anderson, Dr Tom, and Swing, Pam, 1979. *Gie's an A*. University of Stirling.

Graham, John G., and Smith, Brian (eds.), 1995. *Shetland Folk Book, Volume 9*. Shetland Folk Society.

Graham, John G., and Laurence I. (eds.), 1998. *A Shetland Anthology*. Shetland Publishing Company.

Nicolson, James R., 1978. *Traditional Life in Shetland*. Robert Hale.

Robertson, M., 1980. *The Collected Poems of Vagaland*. The Shetland Times Ltd.

Scott, Walter, and Palmer, Richard, 1987. *The flowering plants and ferns of the Shetland Islands*. The Shetland Times Ltd.

Shetland Guild of Spinners, Knitters, Weavers and Dyers, 2012. *A Legacy of Shetland Lace*. The Shetland Times Ltd.

Simpson, Charlie, 2000. *In Da Galley, Sixty essays in seafood philosophy*. The Shetland Times Ltd.

Sutherland, Stella, 1991. *A Celebration and Other Poems*.

Tait, J., and Walterson, F.S. *Island Laughter*.